The
Other Mozart

The
Other Mozart

Poems by
Sharon Chmielarz

Ontario Review Press ✦ Princeton, NJ

Ontario Review Press
9 Honey Brook Drive
Princeton, NJ 08540

Distributed by W.W. Norton & Co., Inc.
500 Fifth Avenue
New York, NY 10110

Library of Congress Cataloging-in-Publication Data

Chmielarz, Sharon.
    The other Mozart / Sharon Chmielarz.—1st ed.
        p. cm.
    ISBN 0-86538-101-1 (alk. paper)
        1. Mozart, Maria Anna Walburga, 1751–1829—Poetry.
    2. Women—Austria—Poetry. 3. Women musicians—Poetry.
    4. Austria—Poetry. I. Title.

PS3553.H57 O84 2001
811'.54—dc21
                                                            00-051503

First Edition

Acknowledgments

Thanks to the editors of the following magazines, where many of these poems were first published, sometimes in earlier forms: *The American Voice:* "Nannerl's Variation on the Smallpox Incident," "Feeling the Way"; *Artworld Quarterly:* "Scenes from Childhood"; *The Beloit Poetry Journal:* "Where She Is: Nannerl Mozart in the Hinterland," "Leopold Mozart: On the Cross"; *Borderlands:* "A Letter from Leopold Mozart to Reassure His Daughter"; *Crab Creek Review:* "The Death of an Archduchess and a Career"; *Cumberland Poetry Review:* "Two Members in the Community," "All I Want"; *Great Midwestern Quarterly:* "Scenes from Childhood"; *Great River Review:* "On Keeping Still"; *The Iowa Review:* "On the Art of Practice," "Tell Her Queen Marie Antoinette Is Pregnant"; *Louisiana Literature:* "What Has She Accomplished Today?"; *The Louisville Review:* "Blackballed"; *Ontario Review:* "If It Be Your Will," "Lorenz Hagenauer…," "The View from Five Octaves," "Fashioning a Single Response," "W. A. Mozart: The Tightrope Walker": *Phoebe,* SUNY: "Bullinger's Offering"; *Prairie Schooner:* "Nannerl Mozart: Speaking of Her Retirement," "Pros & Cons…," "Winter of 1784–85," "The Glass Lady," "Sunning in the Courtyard," "Nannerl Mozart on Names: Trazom"; *Room of One's Own:* "A Visitor to St. Gilgen," "Death of a Dog," "Between Art and Usefulness."

"Nannerl Mozart: "Speaking of Her Retirement," "Pros & Cons…," "Winter of 1784–85," "The Glass Lady," "Sunning in the Courtyard," "Nannerl Mozart on Names: Trazom" reprinted from *Prairie Schooner* by permission of the University of Nebraska Press. Copyright 1999 University of Nebraska Press.

Most of these poems are based on scenes and ideas gathered from or inspired by *The Letters of Mozart and His Family,* translated and edited by Emily Anderson (W. W. Norton & Company, Inc., 1985), *Leopold Mozarts Briefe an seine Tochter,* edited by Erich Otto and Bernhard Paumgartner (Salzburg/Leipzig, 1936), and *Nannerl Mozart* by Eva Rieger (Insel Verlag, Frankfurt, 1990).

My sincere thanks to friends and writing colleagues for their encouragement as I worked on this manuscript. I am indebted as well to staff at the Mozarteum Library in Salzburg; to a Minnesota State Arts Board grant which made research in Austria possible and the writing which followed; to the Anderson Center for a residency. I'd be remiss if I didn't include R C Hildebrandt for her support and Raymond Smith for his interest and editorial care. Thank you all.

Contents

"...dearest Sister... Please trust me absolutely
and never think that I shall forget you;
but remember that things do not always turn out,
or at least not always exactly, as one wishes."

—Wolfgang Mozart (17) to Nannerl, Maria
Anna Mozart (22), March 7, 1778

The
Other Mozart

A WORLD TO CONQUER

All I Want

The way the wolf walks
even within the walls of the city
it's a wonder
as many people live as do.

Money, Nannerl, money is the reason, Papa says.

Moneymoneymoney, the Wunderkinder sing to the king.
Moneymoneymoney, the ironmonger sings to the banker,
the butcher to the brewer, the baker to the joiner.
Wolf is hungry. *Money,*
Wolfgang, money is the reason
to make music, Papa says.

Years of bread and potato
turn the sisters' faces yellow.
Wolf slathers close to the convent,
swallows a peasant in the field instead.
Behind fortress walls the Archbishop eats
all the dumplings his mother sets
before him.

Moneymoneymoney, the wolf sings
over the common grave, over the sarcophagus,
looking for a market. "All I want
is to make music and be rich."

> the sound of
> one student

counting
out two

kreuzers
for the lesson and

the plink
gyring on the music stand.

Between Art and Usefulness

Listen how the iron comes sighing to the clavier:
See how much useful, simple work I've gotten done!
Three of Papa's shirts, his jacket, Nannerl's dress,
white tablecloth, hall curtains, towels, sheets,
the household underpinnings pressed
flat and smooth, white as drone.
And what can you say you've done, Clavier,
standing in your anonymity of uselessness?
How have you pushed the stone?
How have you made it move along
as it does, slug, slug, slug?

On the Art of Practice

"I send greetings to Nannerl and a message urging her to practice hard and to teach little Zezi conscientiously. I know well that she herself will benefit if she accustoms herself to teaching someone else very thoroughly and patiently. I am not writing this without a motive."
—Leopold Mozart, Milan, December 12, 1772

We must all have a quiet place to practice, Zezi.
Even the daughter of the *Zuckerbäcker* practices
in the bakery. Afternoons when the shop's sold out
she swings the door's *"offen"* sign around and takes
a plain brown violin case from under the counter.
Squeak! Squawk! Sh-h-ht! Papa's sleeping—
the early riser, the floury mole stirring dough in the glow
of the oven, Papa, the sweet tooth king, lies upstairs,
rolled in a feathertick. Ruuuuup! he snores. In they go.
Cakes and breads. An hour later, Ruuuup! he snores.
Out they come. Money for violin lessons.
Decorated with chocolate and sweet cherries,
glazed with maple. One day the daughter
wants to be a virtuoso; the shop, a salon
of spindly chairs. During prolonged, difficult,
sour cadenzas customers will savor,
with mincing bites and licking tongues,
Papa's sugary petits fours.

Nannerl's Variation on the Smallpox Incident

"Te Deum Laudamus! Little Wolfgang has got over the smallpox safely!
Now I must give you a few particulars.... The elder son of the goldsmith
with whom we were living, caught smallpox immediately after our arrival
...In vain did I search quickly for another lodging which would take us all.
I was forced to leave my wife and daughter where they were and to run off
with Wolfgang."
                    —Leopold Mozart to Lorenz Hagenauer, November 10, 1767

When the ship is burning the mice do flee.
Before the papa jumps into the water, he
grabs the tail of the choicest morsel, his own
dear *Wundermaus* who smells strongly of gold-
en cheese. No matter how, a safe shore must
be reached. God will provide some *Stück,*
some raft for them to float on.
Or the providence, in danger, to swim.

After they're dry and fed and have slept
in the sailors' inn the two mice begin to cry.
Ah! Poor Those left behind on the ship!
But then a shout from the wharf, they look, they wipe
their wet furry cheeks, they cannot believe their eyes,
the ship, a charcoal hulk, approaches land!
And at the prow two mice in sooty dresses—God be praised—
Mama and Sis—wave to Papa and son, "We made it!"
They knew God was good and would not let two females drown!

Scenes from Childhood

"At Calais I saw how the sea runs away and comes back again."
                              —Nannerl Mozart, April, 1764, Age 12

I'll tell you about Number Seven,
(I was Number Four) how he came slipping
out of Mamma's hole all bloody and screaming.
At eight o'clock, St. Peter's bells counted to eight.
Mamma says I was born at midnight. I got twelve.

We walked to the Cathedral. The sun
made puddles. We gave our bundle to the priest.
He gave it back. All the way home I practiced
saying Seven's name: Johannes Chrysostomus
Wolfgangus Theophilus Mozart. Wolferl.

                    ★

Up the shadowy stairs to Papa's workroom.
Wolferl's the sultan, I'm Roxelana the queen.
We play four hands in the Kingdom of Rücken,
a kingdom of nonsense, a fortress of rhythm.

                    ★

Donnerwetter. Thunder weather. The coach rolls on.
Darkness has never stopped the Wunderkinders' practice.
Papa lays the keyboard on our knees, his face the moon
shining over two heaps of gulden. "Play on, play on."

                    ★

"What's going on in there?" Papa yells, throwing open the door.
"What's happening to my baby?" —Mamma holds Wolferl
close to her breasts. The pitch of his screams drops to a sob.
"It was just a story," I say, hiding Salome Musch under my pillow.
Dolls know about hands, how they wait dead in dust under a bed ...
"Don't you ever frighten your little brother again," Mamma warns.
"Do you want him to die?" Papa says. "He must grow up and support us!"

★

Listen, Wolferl! Your minuet in G,
delicato as lark in filigree.
We played it for the Archbishop,
remember, Wolferl? Old Sigismund?

"Sigismund! Christoph!
Graf von Schrattenbach!"

Stop that barking, you big giggle!
And do you remember that hippo
Fräulein von Guclenus? *"Wolfgang*
Amadè le Mozar!" she oozed.

You wiped her big fat smack
off your cheek, remember?
After our concert in Paris?
Count Zinzendorf raved,

you were *wunderbar.* And I, Wolferl,
was *eine kleine Meisterin,*
a little master. —Wolferl, you
remember, say you do!—

"Sigismund! Christoph!
Graf von Schrattenbach!"

★

The Golden Star, The Three Moors, The Golden Wheel,
The Golden Horn, The Giant's, The Red House,
The Three Kings, Prince Friedrich's, The King of England,
The Golden Lion, The Three Imperial Crowns, The Holy
Ghost, The Golden Dragon, The English Inn, The Gasthof
by the Green Tree, The Black Eagle—and Mamma
rubbing her feet and sighing, "Already six o'clock
and the horses just pulling up to that wretched
inn with its wretched food and wretched bed."

★

"It's only a tiny stream we've just crossed,"
Papa says, retching outside the coach.
"It's nothing, Children, this Maxglanerbach."

"I don't want to travel and get sick!" Wolferl cries.
Papa dabs his lips. "Of course you do, Son!
How else can you be an honest German,

and own a coach and fine clothing?
Never forget, Wolfgang: Money is
the point of music. To make money."

We could sail to America and get rich, I say.
We could play for the natives, Wolferl—I take
his hands—*we would charm them with our music*

and take their cask of gold and give it to Papa,
wouldn't we, Wolferl? And then get another and
play four hands all day and compose concerti.

"Do they have clavichords in America?" Wolferl asks.
"No," Papa says. "Just woods and aborigines."
"Then I don't want to go," Wolferl says.

But we'd own the sea, I tell him. We'd command it,
never to take us back to Salzburg again!
To the Maxglanerbach, a brook which is nothing.

"Drive on!" Papa shouts to Sebastian. We ride on
toward the English Channel, to waves that run away
only to come lapping back to shore to piddle.

★

The dress the Empress gave me—"Maria Antonia's,
too small for the Archduchess, here, you may have it"—
the dress j'adore, white taffeta, material of music,
the dress that flows like moonlight over the Salzach.
"The dress," Papa says, "must be made into a petticoat."
The dress I wear to the sitting (Wolferl wears his gift,
the Archduke Ferdinand's lavender suit with silk socks),
the dress Lorenzoni paints as stocks and sets me in
with my arms and head sticking out. With broad, quick
strokes he makes its light change to match Wolferl's tone.
The dress that shows me, oh how clearly I've been done,
as sister and complementary partner to the Little Plum.

Oma's Little Girl

—from stories Mamma Mozart told Nannerl about Oma Pertl

We lived like mice. Worse than the church mice.
We almost drowned in debt. They took our furniture,
your Oma's savings. All three hundred and fifty gulden
from her first marriage. My sister Rosina and I
sat before empty plates. "How am I going
to feed you two?" your Oma moaned. She took
in sewing. And regretted every noodle and candle
she spent a kreuzer on. And Rosina's casket.

We lived in a tiny tin of a room, the coldest in Salzburg.
When we had firewood I'd warm my rump at the Ofen,
as I used to do in St. Gilgen. Before your Opa died, Nannerl,
we lived in the grandest house on Lake Aber.
Your Opa was the singing prefect, Wolfgang Nikolaus Pertl.
—What nonsense you talk sometimes, Nannerl.
Of course Oma had a name, a beautiful name:
Eva Rosina Barbara Puxbaumer Pertl, née Altmann.

She was living with us when the stork brought you,
after the babies who didn't live, the five the wolf ate up.
Then he took your Oma. That is the way of the wolf. Eat
and shit. Wolves roam the earth, God's home's in heaven.
Your brother's in the music room, run along and play with him.
—Say your name first? Nannerl, you silly goose. You know
your name—Maria Anna Walburga Ignatia Mozart.
Your Oma picked it out. You are Oma's little girl.

Lorenz Hagenauer on Receiving
a Letter from Leopold Mozart

Another letter from Mozart. *Ach, Gott!* Another thick
Long-range directive: "Hagenauer, do this, do that."
I know the content. Even before I open it.
The daughter's playing is brilliant,
The son at twelve has already an imperial commission
But Gluck et al are conspiring against Wolfgang,
Blocking his way to completing his opera,
Blah, blah, blah.
The longer they stay in Vienna the more he/
Leopold needs more of my money.
Would I "... want them to return to Salzburg
In dishonor," these honest Germans?
Ha! A variation on one of his old tactics.
The missive will lie on my table, unopened.
I shall go out into my garden to think
Or not to think about his troubles.
What are they to my *rosa damascena*?

The Death of an Archduchess and a Career

—Maria Josepha's, Vienna, 1767, and Nannerl Mozart's

Every mirror and window
draped in black, the same
mourning as in Lent
after weeks of Carnival.
The family wants no musicians
at the bride's dark wedding,
not even to play a dirge.
They want quiet
servants to tend to their grief.
They want to crawl
into its nest and lie
there half-alive.
They want all the empire
to wear black clothing.
No one will sing or play clavier.
No one will play piquet.
No one will powder the bride-to-be
or decorate her hair with ribbons.
She will take no interest
when old friends call and pay
compliments on her dress,
a pearl-like thing in its trunk,
growing musty and rumpled.
She will spend her honeymoon
underground counting coins
shaped like the sun,

one coin for the eye,
one coin for the tongue,
one coin for her heart.
She will count them again.
Not enough, not enough
to come back for the ring.

The View from Five Octaves

"I am bringing back a book on the antiquities of Verona. Herr von Helmreich... will surely lend you the other two parts of Keyssler, so that, although you are not with us, you can at least travel at home in imagination."
—Leopold Mozart, January 11, 1770

Another tour; Wolfgang promises to come back with lice.
Nannerl and Mamma find new ways to travel at home—
arm in arm, from hearth to hutch, from oven to opera.
Tonight on the steps, they'll hear Hasse. Tomorrow,
on the hob, lunch with the count—Signor Francesco
Eugenio D'Arco. (*Ah, si!* He's heard of *die Mozartin*,
Wolfgang Mozart's *cara sorella, la bella virtuosa*—
Küss Dir die Hand!— whose *Konzert* he awaits—
touching—his lips—to each—of her—soft but firm—
fingertips—*Amor!*) His moustache drips with longing.
Certainly, Keyssler does this house no justice!
Not the shuttered outer walls, nor the inner, home
to keyhooks and washboards, rolling floors and lye-choked
closets. And look! This fine antiquity, Papa's clavichord.
The view from its five octaves is really not to be missed.

16

Years of Exclusion

Nannerl Mozart: Speaking of Her Retirement

"We are as fit as one can be in this dull Salzburg."
                    —Nannerl Mozart, twenty years old

Home. Woman with cat, canary and Bimperl the dog.
With mother and clavier and a shared room:
one of Papa's students sleeps on the red couch
at my bedroom door. I go for long walks.
Merchants smile in passing. They think they have
what I want and there's money for it in my pocket.
—What, Sirs, is the cost of praise?
The devil himself offers an idea.
I send it to Wolferl under my name.
He writes back, "I'm amazed
to find how well you can compose.
In a word, the song is beautiful."
—What is the cost, Sirs, of praise?
The brittle scratch of pen on paper?
A song which dies without a singer?

Nannerl Mozart: BLACKBALLED

"We left Bologna a few days later than we had intended, for by a unanimous vote [three white balls] the Accademia Filarmonica received Wolfgang into their society and awarded him the diploma of Accademico Filarmonico."
—Leopold Mozart, Milan, October 20, 1770

In the Accademia Filarmonica of the Hannibalplatz
the judges are entering the kitchen, they are nodding,
they are beaming, they are saying they have waived
unwritten requirements and award me the Diploma
in the Grossa Hoopla of the Hearth: This sets me free
from a duke's whims and folly, from the double
curse of promotion and dickering over first chair,
from rivalries between singer and oboist,
from the tedium of *après Konzert*, the glitz
of diamond rings (and the necessary silk
to keep the king's around my little finger),
from the quandry of indecision—moiré
or taffeta?— from the bustle of the theater
and the danger on the road, from robbers
of compositions and problems with a script,
from the envy of my colleagues, German & Italian,
from the copyist's tricks and rain-soaked luggage,
from snowy roads and stinking inns, cold beds and
thin soups, and, at the end of my performance, from
the roar of silence before the hall cracks into applause.

Getting Wet

"When things fare well or badly with you, think of us, who are obliged to live sadly here, separated from you both."
　　　　　—Nannerl Mozart to Wolfgang and Mamma in Paris

Overhead, rolls of lard-colored clouds.
Lightning splits, dousing Salzburg
with the stench of sulphur.
Afternoon darkens to dinge.
In the downpour housegutters
gush like troops of beerdrinkers
peeing hard and long on stone.
Anyone in the inn, at the window,
sees a young woman, slim, tall,
in a black felt hat walking her terrier
down a lane, both caught, sadly,
in rain. Anyone watching her
sees how sorrow clings.

Giving Tresel Fair Warning

"Our maid Tresel finds it extraordinarily funny that Nannerl should be for-
ever...scolding her daily about [the kitchen's] dirty condition..."

—Leopold Mozart

Laughs when I tell her the floor begs
someone to get down on her hands
and knees and scrub. Says I scream
at twenty-six just like old market women.
Says she doesn't recognize a stinky
blob stuck to the floor, that it is something
the dog dragged in. Goes vacant when
I yell, *Surely not Bimperl since you never
let her out.* Is not impressed
when I tell her Old Mitzerl, next door,
watches from the upstairs window
and thinks I should let Tresel go—
"She does noszink. All day, noszink."
Smirks. Makes a joke of work.
Widens her eyes like a prima donna
of klatsch when I tell her her little habit
of lying—yes, lying—does not help
her position in this house one bit.
Stubborn. A forehead like iron. Doesn't
even listen to me.

Tresel: On the Mozarts

Ash Wednesday. Gray skies and hangover
and soot in the pots. The pay here is miserable.
Though she likes working for them, says Tresel;
no pigsty to clean. And she's deaf in the left ear
so she doesn't mind their constant practice.
Frau Mozart and the daughter help iron and dust.
There're plenty of forks and spoons; with the men
away, concerting, only two mouths to feed at the table.
Back home there were eighteen around the bowl
and one spoon. And a stove where Tresel fought
with Mother—whether to keep the lid on during the boil
or leave it off. Pay here is miserable, says Tresel,
but she does what she wills; she leaves the lid off.

The Shape of Music

A note is a shard
Of a thought. A line
Is a piece to the handle.
An adagio is a vessel
From which one
Idea flows.
An allegro, a shell
For another.
A sonata fills
With octaves
Of mood
And opinion.
Our trembling
And faltering
Are broken
Bits from the basin.

Tell Her Queen Marie Antoinette Is Pregnant

—snippets from Frau Mozart's last letters to Leopold Mozart and Nannerl, 1778

We've arrived by mailcoach, nearly choked by wind and drowned
    by rain
but safe and sound, praise and thanks be to God.

Wolfgang is bored, he hasn't gotten a clavier yet, and the hall
is so narrow it will be impossible to have one brought up.

My own life is not at all a pleasant one. I sit alone in our room the
    whole day long
as if I were in jail, so dark in here I couldn't possibly know what the
    weather is like.

And for this we pay thirty livres a month.
Lunch is calf's foot in some dirty sauce.

By the way, Baron de Grimm paid a visit; you're not to worry
    so much,
shit in your bed and make it crack. Everything comes out right in
    the end.

Madame d' Épinay's given me her red satin gown and fan!
Though indeed I cannot understand one word of her language.

How is Frau Adlgasser doing? Barbara Eberlin? Does she still pay you
    visits?
Does Nannerl teach at Andretter's every week as usual?

Tell Nannerl the frisure they wear here is extraordinarily high all
    round,
more than a foot. Tell her Queen Marie Antoinette is pregnant.

I had a real good laugh over your letter for I know the girl Sigmund
    Haffner's engaged to,
the daughter of the brewer at Uttendorf. She looks older than her
    twenty-six,
but only because she was worked to death at the Colonel's.
    A charming match for Sigmund.

Herr Raaff comes to see us almost daily.
He calls me "Mother" and sings me arias;
I am quite in love with his voice.

I walked in the Luxembourg Gardens and into the Palace's picture
    gallery;
was frightfully tired when I got home. Alone. Wolfgang's lunching
    with Raaff.

As to the lightning conductor, I can't find out what people here
    think about it,
as I don't know the language. It seems to me God can find anybody
    He wants and no lightning conductor can save him.

Nannerl Mozart: Fashioning a Single Response

"I hope, my queen, that you are enjoying…health and that now and
then…you will sacrifice for my benefit some of your important and intimate
thoughts…."
—Wolfgang Mozart to Nannerl, Vienna, August 14, 1773

I hope, my sensitive ass, that you receive my sacrifice
pawing, pouncing, snorting and horsing around in courts
and/or any other low place where His Highness allows
idle tongues to wag begging for thoughts—yours,
like any ass's, come at the end where an asinine
demand traditionally & charitably exists
though marginally on a page; namely, in the P.S.,
a flatulent last blast which you, dear Arse,
were so wont to deliver in the practice room—
crepidos ventris which resembled the squall
from a brass section squatting on a hill
of Bavarian dung. My dear little Beetlebomb,
even the stoutest nose (how related the word
nose is to noise!) would have flinched, as do
equine-nostriled Viennese when they possess
during feverish *Sommerhitze* an especially keen sense
of smell and source, and where a prodigious horn
like yours is small advantage—I digress, however,
from fulfilling your request. Enclosed lie two intimate
thoughts for my donkey monkey, the little A-hole
in a cherry red suit, the great *Wunder Arse* at the keyboard,
der Herr Dr. Wiggly Butt in the parlor but not the boudoir
(or? yet?), the twin to my own brown braying heart. No. 1:
Shit in your bed and make a good mess. No. 2: Remember
the sad smell of your own sweet queen, Lick My Arse.

I Want a Man

—Nannerl's friend the chambermaid, Katherl Gilowsky

Poor Katherl. Chasing after every man.
Katherl couldn't catch a man if he were

sizzling in a frying pan.
The butt of whispered conversation.

And that Kostüm of hers.
She has worn it to rags.

And her own voice sighing as she poses
in the mirror as *la Madame*—"I want a man,

Nannerl. In autumn. When the sun shines
white and thin as the Komtessa's hand."

Can she help the crumbs she earns at Firmian's?
Or having a head for Tarot, ribbons and easy

one-pot, *Eintopf,* meals? And wanting
a marriage to house them all in? After all, she

doesn't have a famous brother, hasn't traveled
all over the world. Can't give clavier lessons.

Doesn't want to live off her brother Franz Wenzel
or her sister Josepha. Then she'd really

chew her nails, pale moons graced by bleeding.
What man was ever lured by blood?

Nannerl Mozart on Names: Trazom

"I do hope that Wolfgang will make his fortune in Paris quickly...."
—Mamma Mozart, 1777

God's will. God's time. A long time
before fame and fortune, Wolfgang.
Maybe Big Money comes slowly
because you're always riding away
from us, off to Munich, to Paris,
to lunch at Count Blah's house.
And when you use an alias—Gnagflow
Trazom—God can't find you.

If only we knew which language He loves best!
Wolfgang, when you pray beside your bed
say your name clearly. Remind God
in French— Amadè, in Latin— Amadeus,
in Greek—Theophilus, in Italian—Amedeo,
in German—Gottlieb, that He, above all, loves you.

An Honorable End

—for Leopold Mozart's old friend

Anton Weiser's troubles are over.
His breath grew heavy in the evening,
at eight o'clock he went into eternity.
An honorable man, this old friend.

After the Requiem (Michael Haydn
at the organ; Mozart behind the baton)
a few of Weiser's old friends
intoned their own benediction.

In the music hall the Sauter boy
fiddled through the *clunk* of steins.
Haydn roared, "Another round!"
No one wanted to go home.

Out the windows till past one
roomlight tumbled onto snow.
Trapped, it burned the alley gold,
having nowhere else to go.

Bullinger's Offering

"...sad and distressing news.... My dear mother is very ill."
—Wolfgang Mozart to his father, Paris, July 3, 1778

"All I ask of you at present is to act the part of a true friend, by preparing my poor father very gently for this sad news [Frau Mozart's death]. I have written to him by this post, but only to say that she is seriously ill..."
—Wolfgang Mozart to Abbé Bullinger in Salzburg, Paris, July 3, 1778

Out of the world
we lived in last week,

                safe

if that unlocked room
holds nothing

                Bullinger

hands us a shrouded offering:
Mamma isn't ill

                but

dead in Paris.
What we have

                suspected

from the silence
between

                Wolfgang's

hem and hawing,
his hand's

                              draping
  words in black,
  in shapeless

                              cloth.

Leopold Mozart: On the Cross

Don't alibi for him, Nannerl. It isn't the Archbishop.
Wolfgang wants to be rid of me, his own father, his teacher,
his one true friend. The old man is useless, throw
the work and suffering and sacrifice to the wind.

God only knows how Wolfgang will pay
for nailing me to this cross. But he will. Debts of
honor and duty; over one thousand gulden
squandered while your dear mother was alive.

God forgive us all she died, chaperoning him,
alone, sick, in a stinking Parisian hotel room,
bled insufficiently, on a fast day. And Wolfgang
pays the bleeder for it after she's died!

In the very next letter he's mentioning that
slut Aloisia Weber. He will "make her career."
Make *her* career! The puffed-up *Gogelkopf*.
The meathead! I tell you, I get so angry...

chi va piano, va sano, I tell him. Who goes slowly
goes sanely. But not Wolfgang. No. Luck
is with him. In Vienna he will make us at least
a thousand a year. Ha! A thousand promises.

He's sending me a stick, Nannerl, a walking stick
that I should "use instead of him and always
carry it." I could break it. I could break the back
of this house with it had he not already broken

mine. Oh, Nannerl, he will eat his words.
And we, hapless, misguided mice shall starve
with him. Under the eye of the Arch Lummox,
long-toothed, laughing on his Mönchsberg throne.

"Improvisator!" he called me once. The name
rolled down to my feet. Yes. I improvise a rock
to build my house on, and it turns into a walking
                                              stick.

Punishing the Deceiver

"Tell Spitzeder that if he wants to meet his former impresario Crosa, he can find him in Milan, where he goes about begging, miserably clad and with a long beard. Thus it is that God punishes deceivers."
—Leopold Mozart

On "the day the great blessing took place"
—Wolfgang's phrase for his marriage to Constanze—
Abbé Bullinger stops by to visit the deceived:
Nannerl, queen of the lace her brother sends
to the tower, a tax on his conscience, and
Papa, whose mind swings from stalk to thorn

to the two-armed cross of impatience and
lust on which his son has nailed his future.
Though greed doesn't make the tree a trinity,
for the little woman is as poor as the beggars
Herr Mozart & Son most surely will become—
sackclothed, shuffling down the empire's lanes,

beggar cup in hand. Addled Leopold
and the King of Blackguards, their mouths
full of humble pie and peacock feathers.

How patiently Abbé Bullinger tags after!
Picking the old man's gnarled thoughts out
of the son's hair, thorn by mourning thorn.

Found Poem: The Unmarried Daughter

Who will buy it, Papa asks.
For whom would it be right?

Who has such a small waist, compact body?
Who can pay that much for it? Eighteen gulden!

Who wants it, since it's out of date?
Not the seamstress in the Lodron shop—

it's been taken in too many times.
And the fabric's full of needle pricks.

Nevertheless, Papa says,
he'll try to sell my bodice.

If It Be Your Will

"[Nannerl] gets up daily at six o'clock and goes to Holy Trinity, where she prays so ardently that several people have already spoken to me about it."
—Leopold Mozart

I notice it evenings. When we play four hands,
Herr Gott, Papa's dressing gown, a rag, reeks of
nervousness, the sweat of the round-shouldered

Lazarus in hell, smoldering in black wool Berlin
stockings. "You won't starve," Papa says, patting
my arm, thinking I fear the future, the domestic

service the Prince requires of all unmarried
daughters. "Even if your penniless father
dies and you can't count on your brother."

Papa says I am working very hard,
there is no one with more "perfect insight."
No one who can "extemporize so successfully."

No one who smiles so bravely
as she sells her lovely English hat and
the Elector's gift, the galanterie set of bottles

for fifty florin. So dear. The amount St. Hubert
spent on a hunting dog in one season.
A puny bit, a pretense of weight in a tin. Yes,

I'll send it to Wolfgang, though it is mine,
though the debt is huge, even eight hundred
florin would be no windfall, though Wolfgang's

life is all gypsies and soldiers, though his
answers to letters arrive like Yours,
Herr Gott, overwhelming—or not at all.

Captain d'Ippold

"I should very much like to know how things are progressing between you and a certain good friend, you know whom I mean. Do write to me about this! Or have I lost your confidence in this matter?"

—Wolfgang to Nannerl, Vienna, 1781

I would like to go after his neck. Something about
     nesting a kiss
in the hollow of a neck, especially if the man has
     quite unfastened
his lace jabot and black cravat. There is something
     about the way
a neck roots into a chest. Such a man I could
     nuzzle, embrace,
close my eyes to, lick and nip his chin; could lay
     my head against
a bastion of ruffles and buttons, an attar of bones and
     hirsute incense.
Have I fallen in love, Amadè? I could sleep or fly
     on bull in lace.

Death of a Dog

Tresel: Tresel has always shaken her head at the Mozarts—
townspeople who keep an animal, a dog in the house.
And now the dog has died on a hot July afternoon.
The sky threatens showers, and the Mozarts expect
Tresel to dodge lightning bolts to dig a dog's grave.

Papa: Tresel and Nannerl carry the shovels. I push
the barrow down the street. Bimperl's body,
wrapped in a blanket, bumps to every cobble en route
to the willows. After a life of wagging, the tail that did
for tongue is quiet; obedient as ever to God's will.

Nannerl: A woman gawks at our procession. *A lonely job,*
she says. We nod. My heart aches.
And I'm glad when it begins to rain.
We lower Bimperl's body into her grave,
we begin to fill the hole in.

A Marriage of Convenience

Pros & Cons: A Marriage of Convenience

—Nannerl Mozart to the Prefect, Johann Baptist von
Berchtold zu Sonnenburg, Freiherr/Baron

If only he were English!
(She loves the English.)
If only he had come

from
anywhere else
but St. Gilgen

flashing his title, his house, his stability. His money
sucking up her bankruptcy, her virginity, the shreds
of her former glory

and guaranteeing her
four hours daily practice.
Papa approves. And pushes.

And she? Well, she's
thirty-three; he's forty-eight;
he may die first.

The Bride's New Home

Welcome to St. Gilgen—which is long
On fishnets, crabs, chickens, rabbits,
Sausage, tame duck and wild duck,
Mutton, lard, wool. And wood, lumber
For window shutters. Gilgeners import
All chocolate, leeks, books, soap,
Lemon, sugar, tooth powder, paper,
Shoes, hats—felt or straw—
Mustard, saffron, starch, thread—
Silk or cotton—camomile, clavichord strings,
Candles, wine vinegar, salve for burns,
Shaving brushes, lentils, almond paste
Make-up, tobacco, rice, brooms, calendars
For the Archbishop's court, caraway sweetened
Sauerkraut, peppermint, hair powder, music,
Salt—in short, any luxury they can think of.

From the shops in Salzburg, from the market
In the square under Trinity's dome, these wares
Bump like brides in wagon beds through the east
Stone gate of Salzburg, thirty kilometers, six hours
South over stonehorn eruptions, dragon humps
And chamois skulls to St. Gilgen, a village
Where peony heads rust at garden gates.
This one by the lake is the widowed prefect's.
His cook and five children run out to the wagon,
Lug the treasure, straw clinging like angel hair,

Across the flagstone to back door and larder
Where cook lifts each package from a child's
Arms, stacks it on the shelf, pats the last
Rustle in place before locking the pantry door.
How sweetly each ware garnishes the meal
Served that night on the bridegroom's wooden table.

Two Members in the Community of St. Gilgen

The priest,
pregnant under his robes
with the delight of wine's early afternoon,
marvels at the turn of each season, how each is
a time just deliciously long enough to make
the barley and rye and wheat he consecrates
and turns to light during Advent and Christmas
and doles out like rations during the starved darkness.
He hiccups and thinks no one hears.
To anyone kneeling at the railing it's clear
he's drinking in the sacristy where his vestments
hang from hooks and smell sour as the room,
the priest, and walls of St. Aegidius.
Guzzle and dawdle. No need to rush
into the coming night.

And the peasant
walking along the black
furrow, eyes the hole where she'll
drop the potato.
All will be well if...
Soil and rain be good.
Sprout grows down through ground.
Sun stirs tuber to round
and bulge with fruit,
the eye's/ earth's/ meat.
Her task, to stoop and drop.
Her back, her brain, her eye, her leg,
her hand, her heart all eager to obey the empty
stomach's command.

The Bridegroom

In the round mirror, the face of morning triumph.
Herr Husband for the third time, the Prefect of St. Gilgen,
has shot some stars into the dark and smothered them
in a feathertick, not nearly two warm meters wide, an opus
of a mattress where the King of the Honeymoon reigns.

Now he is doing his hair.
Brushing and powdering and ribboning. Rocking
on his heels. Thick sensuality pursed on his lips.

He has it, the marriage contract's sheet-spot,
a bloody *Kleck* worth 500 gulden, a virgin ruby
in his three-stone collection. Plus five children.

The children. Unlike the peasant, the Prefect has
no fields to work them in. He has but one desk, one son
would fit it nicely. So the rest must be God's gifts—

ranging, loudly, from ages thirteen to two,
on the wedding day, yesterday, making a ruckus
for the bride in brown at the altar in St. Aegidius.

"Quiet!" the uncles had bellowed, delivering ear tweaks
and knuckle thumps. Onkel Joseph Sigismund (the drunkard).
Onkel Johann Nepomuk (the wife-beater). *"Mal ruhig! Quiet!"*
The priest, hard of hearing, proceeded—

a bother, love being exempt from a prefect's
obligations. Like trees, the children are tossed

in storm till quiet, caressed by a wind called *Föhn,*
rooted to the father only for food and water. Look

again. Was there some face he should gaze into
deeply? In order to see, more clearly, his own?
Each minute in the Prefect's house is huge!

Nannerl Mozart's Marriage: No Place to Hide

He, the blond in the parlor,
thin-haired Herr Spouse

in opposite chair. I, the brunette,
my high coiffure a colony

of cotton rats. *Der Herr*
throws a special glance

from his place to mine,
the span of a yoke.

His eyebrows scold.
His son told lies and stole

sugar for pranks.
My fault.

A featherbed offers seclusion,
a cushiony retreat from that room.

How rude then for him
to follow, to find me,

to slide in. In tandem,
this duty and lust.

Signs of War

"Have you heard, dear Daughter, about the Massacre in the *Siebengebirgen*?
Your husband, our *Herr Sohn*, will surely worry it, pore over it in the
papers. It is not something to fear. What can we do about war?"
                                    —Leopold Mozart, Salzburg, December, 29,1784

What can we do about the Tsarina,
billowing across the Crimea, scattering
Turks like jacks? Hooves splatter the map
with mud. "Dammit, You Stuckers, charge!"

Halt! Here we must praise the Archbishop.
Hieronymus reduces a drunken soldier's
punishment from *opera seria*—a firing squad—
to a bloody flogging in the square.

As for the emperor, Kaiser Josef diddles
at his desk, thinking *kaiserliche* thoughts—
"Bavaria? For a piece of Holland?" "No
way!" chorus King Friedrich and the Dukes,

"it is stupid! *Verrückt!* We will resist."
—With boys. *Schöne Jungs!*
Beautiful boys. Mothers' butterflies.
All suited up to make war. Who can help

guessing at the cost of their outfits? Spotless
pants. *Blitz-blank!* Jackets red as blood

and bankruptcy. The Duke's generous
to a fault. The cobbler's purse swells.

His and the smith's and the butcher's.
Joiner is the one who loses;
how can he sell a coffin when the boys
wind up en masse in a ditch?

Nannerl: Could Have Been

"I'm sorry you didn't get to hear her [Regina Strinasacchi, violinist and guitarist], a great, pleasing, about 23 years old, not indecent and very talented wench."

—Leopold Mozart to Nannerl, Salzburg, December, 1785

I am ill again, sick, sick. I could have been
I could have been I could have been
just a little sick. And twenty-three. And
not indecent—a Regina Strinasacchi
whose whole heart and soul shines
in the adagio as she pulls the melody
across her bow. Just so, her tone
and the strength of the tone.
"Yes, a wench with talent
plays with more expression than a man."

This is the threat life poses.
Obscurity or praise. Cramps or fever.
Camomile with eggwhite. Beer
in barley water: *Gerstenschleim.*
If the monthlies, the *Ordinari,* don't come,
do nothing or send Barisani a sample of urine.
Ambition or health. My health, Papa says,
is the most important thing now I've got.

Winter of 1784–85

Cattle stand hungry in the snow,
their ribs like pitchfork tines.
The *Wienerblättchen* reports the road
to Linz is blocked. As is St. Gilgen's.

In every corner stands the iron
rod of cold. In the yard, dogs
scavenge in a pile of trash—frozen
fish guts and menstrual rags.

Beams insure the house
won't cave in under the weight
of a second story and the eight
stairways, the narrowest, a chute

to the kitchen, to stove and churn Cook
hides behind. "Anything wrong, Mum?"
—In the hall opposite Mamma's portrait
Kaiser Joseph II frowns down.

The Kachelofen warms the parlor
and *Ofensitzer*—children and father.
Six tin-eared Gilgeners on the bench.
Warders of one pregnant Salzburger.

The Clomper in the Prefect's House

How worthy she is of being called old
lumbering Martha. But it's too late
for him to bow out; to his neighbors
he'd be the cad who left his wife
pregnant, alone, to scrounge
for herself. She tells him she has
washed his shirt and hung it up
his way, straightened her drawer
and polished the shoescuffs which
irritate him. He grunts at these
incidents taking place before
the gate to her wall. She sees
he doesn't see his silence
at the table, or the gesture
she just made at her chin,
her response to a comment he's taken
from the standard conjugal list
nailed to his forehead.

Where She Is: Nannerl Mozart in the Hinterland

Where she is, her clavier is
unstrung in the practice room overlooking
the frozen lake. Papa knows it, he and the repairman
will come and fix it but
it's the getting out there in February, "... no fun
being thrown around in an open car
for six hours in cold and wind."

Don't I know it, Papa!

Where she is, the 30th of March is now
impossible. In Salzburg, Papa is
busy with Gluck's *Orfeo.*
But yes, yes, he'll come as soon as he can.

Understand, I have no instrument out here to play, Papa!

Papa knows that, but at least four
rehearsals with music are needed,
and Papa and Gluck *must* be present.
Ditto Herr Altmann the librettist,
who can't be left on his own,
he doesn't know how to write poetry or edit.

Heading toward April now
where she is. After Easter?
Whenever Papa's free,
the repairman isn't.

I am without music, Papa, hours
drag through the house—
what if I sent Berchtold's coach?

That won't help; schedule's
too tight. What she needs
to practice is patience.

Of course, Papa. Come when you can.

A Baby from the Baroness, Nannerl Mozart

Mine is the child
born in the music master's house,
home to children spinning
skeins of song from straw and flax.

Mine is the child
left behind for my father,
a namesake for the little man
dancing around the cradle—

Such perfect fingers!
And the way the hand falls
in sleep. A born clavierist! This one
will spin a gold mountain.

My little Leopold, my son,
my first-born planted like a talent,
my excuse to return
to the spin-wheel's music.

A Letter from Leopold Mozart to Reassure
His Daughter That All Is Well

I've already told you, Nannerl, your departure
was sweetened only by your son's staying.
We like little Leopold, he pleases us
especially after he stops bawling.
Be assured we are getting used to him.
Even the diapering end of it. Even the pissing
when Nanny changes him. Straight up in her face!

Yes, the fever persists; his tongue's blistered.
He can't eat. His stool reeks, and his butt is
chafed. But his wind is strong. I had the honor
yesterday after supper to experiment:
I lifted our little pink piggy by the ankles
and an unbroken salvo of farts fired over his crib:
Proficiat! Prosit, conducat sitque salut!

I'm returning the nipple and baby bottle; sucking
sugarwater from the nanny's finger will do—
you and Wolfgang are proof of it. Don't worry!
I'll stay home till he's well—in case Nanny leaves
to visit her sister. Be glad little Leopold is here.
Be grateful for your Papa! Now you have more time
to look after your husband's other five children.

For Nannerl Mozart's Son, Leopoldl,
and His Sore Throat

—St. Blaise Day, February, 1786

For supper it's trout,
a present from the fishes
under the bridge, nice white flakes
Grandpapa has searched with a fork
to find mean bones. And still one catches
in your throat like a hook.

Mama isn't there to hear the fuss
and watch the flush spread over your face.
So Grandpapa shushes you—Eat, eat!
Butterbread will soothe the sting. Yes?
Now we'll get you blessed at Loreto.
All will be well. Alright, Leopoldl?

The cobblestones are slick on the lane
to the chapel. Grandpapa won't let you down
from his arms till you're in, in the line
swaying and shuffling to the altar. St. Blaise?
Not the real saint, Grandpapa whispers,
the real is invisible though present.

You see him anyway, bobbing toward you,
a sandman with crossed candles,
strewing shadow from his sleeves. *Sleep,*
Leopoldl, sleep, the linen murmurs.
All night you'll glide over hooks in the Salzach,
safe in a boat made of blessing.

Moon of the Bride to Convenience

On June 5, 1786, Nannerl Mozart attended Emanuel Schikaneder's play *Der Grandprofos* with her husband, father, and Katherl Gilowsky, chambermaid & old friend.

How old the moon is!
How many times it's rolled
mid-proscenium, lighting
one head bobbing toward another's

lips, and the snatched kiss is
all *forte* and *piano* and
singing in ranges otherwise
unreachable.

How old the moon is,
this June moon. A woman
in a dark house pretending
she is the sun in the night.

A Gift for Nannerl Mozart from Her Former Sweetheart

In the dead of winter a crate,
packed in straw, jiggles in a wagon
bound for the outback of St. Gilgen and
arrives at the Prefect's gate. His children

swarm around it. Their stepmother
wields a crowbar and the slat's nails shriek—
one heft exposes yellow apples in nests
and the rose blush that caresses each.

Take me, the gift says, *eat me. But please*
send something back in the crate. Anything.
The Captain couldn't stand to pry it open, to find
only an icy note from you signed "Madame."

Over dessert, she tells her husband about the gift.
He agrees it would be proper to reciprocate.
Husband isn't jealous. Of apples. Or the defeated.
Between him and love lie miles of empty space.

A Visitor to St. Gilgen Comes and Goes

While on holiday the Huber girl drops in.
She brings me, *die Mozartin*, a letter from Papa
before she catches the next coach back

to Salzburg. Her sweetheart's busy there,
directing theater; he says she may stay
in St. Gilgen till Ascension. But one day is long

enough, though she's enjoyed the cup
of coffee at the *Weisses Rössl,* and the visit
to the Glass Shack in Zinkenbach,

and the view over Lake Aber
from the *Falkensteinwand,* hawk's cliff,
where St. Wolfgang duped the devil.

After she leaves, her ribbons awhirl,
I read Papa's letter—he sends
to the outback kisses

for the "alabaster hands"
he gave away. The X's lie
in the ash of his remorse.

What Has She Accomplished Today, Besides Counting?

—for Nannerl Mozart abandoned in St. Gilgen, 1787

1

As the hour or minute or day requires,
a woman can count while holding her tongue.
Eleven. Twelve. Thirteen, done!
When she counts she needn't think:
About Papa, the pleated bed caps she's sewn
and he won't wear; about her son on his name day.
"What a fine embroidered cap!" Old Mitzerl will sigh
leaning over his crib. "Such a splendid coat. What
a shiny silver *Taler.* Such beauty-full red shoes,
such fine red shoestrings, Little Leopold!
From the Mama, stuck out in St. Gilgen?"

2

For the bride who wears a kitchen chain,
seven kilos of chickenfeed. With her right arm
she scatters it, with her left she dances with a bear,
the seventy-year-old bridegroom at her wedding.
By Papa's count her period should start today.
Outside it's snowing and nine below. Good:
Her heated nature makes her sweat and keeps her thin.
Staying cool must be her number one concern.

3

At her feet, one broad expanse of frozen lake
with view of bleached reeds and mountains.
In her mind, Carnival costumes and confetti,
Salzburg's are humble compared to Munich's,
but Amazonian under the sound of February
snow falling through the silence of St. Gilgen.

A Cook for Nannerl

> "Aren't there any decent people anymore?"

Papa calls Nannerl's ex "the cold eyeball."
His latest, referred by Frau Schirkoferin, is

Veronika, a born servant. Makes roastbeef
á la rock. In her clean golden Linzer cap, she

drags one foot but can walk fast to market.
She feeds him like a soldier: If there's something

on hand he eats; if not, he doesn't.
Another cook who won't last.

"Aren't there any decent people
anymore?" writes Nannerl to Papa

as she squeezes all her worldly baggage
down into a podunk and turns her

self into eternal-virgin matron,
twin to the Countess Kletzl who's

also lost a cook and can't find another,
decent one. Improvisation in a kitchen.

Straw to the Court's elegant corruption.
A martyr of all sorts, under the foot of

children and the neighbors, those proud
cluckers, not one with more than two

kreuzers in their hearts... which leads
back to Nannerl's actually getting

a cook in St. Gilgen. As Papa says,
"Who would want to go out there?"

The Glass Lady

Glassware and bottles. That's what I hauls.
And personal delivery service if you miss the postal coach.
Regular: Once a week between St. Gilgen and Salzburg.
That's how I met the Mozarts. The Mister in Salzburg,
the Daughter in St. Gilgen. *Ja,* and if I had just one kreuzer
for every time I've driven the wagon up to Number 8
—the old Tanzmeister's house in the Hannibalplatz—
and the package for the Daughter wasn't ready—
"A minute, a minute!" he snipes. I glares. Why not?
As if it's my fault he's late!
Herr Fuss and Clamor storms about the room.
Herr Bustle von String and Scissor.
Such an old man. "Take your time," I tells him.
"It's your money lost, if something gets broken."
He cinches his bundles with double knots.
I gives the old codger my highest praise,
"You would've made a good shipper."

Everything from duck to broken clavichord string
the Daughter sends him. "Don't lose it," she says, pulling
on my sleeve. I hates it when they pull on my sleeves.
"I never lose wares," I mutters. "Not if they're packaged good."
And would I want to steal her fishy-smelling clavichord string?
She thinks I'm running short?
"No, Mum," I says, bunching her packages down good
into the wagonbed, between bottles and straw.
"It's important," she says. — What they all say.—
"It's the lake," she says. "Strings snap. Then I can't play."
Oh, I knows what snaps in the Prefect's house. Cook tells me.
It's in the marriage contract, don't you know: Four hours a day

the wife plays. The five kids go wild in the house.
Their racket floats out the windows with her music and the Prefect's
voice, tighter than a knot: "Someone keep them QUIET!" —
Cook says she's played for the King of England Himself.
She gets no raves from me; if I don't haul, she don't play.

A Blue Note

The success of other women musicians:
Regina Strinasacchi, Nancy Storace. The established
Josepha von Auernhammer, Maria Theresia von Paradis,
Madame Bitzenberg, the damned Davies sisters.
Even Constanze Weber, that two-bit squeaking
field mouse, procured a solo at St. Peter's.
Only because of Wolfgang! The list lengthens,
a struggle against envy. Therese Friberth.
Gretl Marchand, her latest three sonatas.
Carnival has been a fairyland of awards for her—
a shower of earrings, pendants, pearls, bracelets,
Count von Seeau's gifts to the brilliant sixteen-year-old
who is *so* at home with the new pianoforte.
"You'd like the touch, Nannerl," she writes,
"it's *so* easy to play. I could show you how in a minute."

Found Poem: Leopold Mozart to His Daughter

Tresel is with me.
I'm not well. Not at all. Not getting better.
Thin. A wind could blow me from life.
Enclosed are the candles you need.
Unbelievable, how expensive they are.
This box, 15 kreuzer.
Captain d'Ippold visits me daily.
Little Leopold is fine.
I'm spending so much on medicine I can't afford
to pay Mitzerl next door the 45 gulden I owe her
so if our Herr Son could pay her?
Your brother's moved. Again. Now
his address is
Landstrasse, # 224.
He wrote me but there was nothing
of consequence in his letter. Absolutely
empty of it. I fear the reasons.

You Know How Papa Practices

Death is "our truest friend... the true goal of our existence... the key that
unlocks the door to happiness.... Tell me the whole truth, or get someone
to write it to me... I'll come to your arms."
—Wolfgang to Leopold, April 14, 1787

He's propped up on pillows, Wolfgang,
slurping and hardly raising his eyes from
the spoon. Of soups he prefers barley or rice
with a little veal or beef, just enough, he says,
to keep his feet on earth. He talks of theater,
as if he still could walk across the square.
"A lonely man likes to watch the women
who like a place to parade."
He tells me you've moved again,
to #224 Landstrasse.
I let it go at that. This time neither of us
mentions your difficulties with creditors.
Papa tells me to take little Leopold, my son,
back to St. Gilgen. He's your unrivaled replacement,
Wolfgang; letting him go augurs the end.
Tresel rattles about with her sick-bed trays.
In the hall she gives me her assessment.
"It's time, Mum, time for him to shit in his pants
and die. Give the rest of us peace in the hours
we have left. Tresel says, 'Get the man on to heaven.' "
Papa lies white as the tick he wraps himself in—
you know how Papa practices for everything, Wolfgang,
even the coffin. Eyes open, Papa looks resigned
to go through its door, with or without the arms
you almost offer.

One Less Worry

—Tresel the maid to Nannerl on Leopold Mozart's death

She can't deny, she's relieved he's passed on.
One less worry. One less room.
She'll shake out his pockets, with luck
eight gulden may turn up, enough to pay
Tresel what's due her. But she can't
stay on, Mum. She hears him all night.
All night his scrounging goes on. His steps
slip-slap, felt *Pantoffel* cross the parquet.
He checks the saltbox, click-clack,
double-shuts the lid tight. His voice,
hoarse, curses last Sunday's beef,
boiled till Tresel was sure it was tender.
As he let her know then and does not relent
in re-telling: She has overcooked again.
So busy directing, he can't leave for heaven.
Eight gulden, Mum, then Tresel'll be gone.

Nannerl Mozart: On Surfacing from Sleep

Who in the dream
is the young, good-looking woman?
A wife to shadow? She slips
in and out of slumber, fires
the watchman and retires the maid
who dries before her eyes
and blows away like savings.
Rattle, scuttle across flagstone—
mummy-music outside the music room.

My second child, Jeanette, is born.

*

The pock-marked priest
unlocks the mystery,
lifts the brass dome to the *Taufbecken,*
dips his hand
into the basin where holiness is
sleeping. He wakes the water
for the lion's blessing
and marks my child,
three drops on her forehead.

How she screams!

Playing Four Hands with Wolfgang

—In Memoriam: Nannerl Mozart on her brother's death

Wolferl, Wolferl,
what are we going to do with you!

> *They forgot, the rats! She*
> *got sick. The coach was*

What have we done to you?
What will happen to you—so
sweet, so ravenous?

> *late. The Count implored and*
> *I had to stay. The King*

You will eat us alive.
We will eat you alive.

> *of Prussia himself was there*
> *and demanded it of me. The*

Have eaten you alive.

> *weather was foul, the wheel*
> *fell off. We couldn't*

Boy wonder, stuck in the elephant's
basket and paraded under a canopy

> *get horses. The time was*
> *not ripe. The prima donna*

in the land of flesh-eating
pygmies. *Wunder* sized-up
as a one-swallow meal.

> *failed miserably, the old*
> *cow. The inn was too*

Wolferl, sweet Jack Pudding,
Sultan of the Kingdom of Rücken,

> *expensive but the town*
> *was full, what else, Nannerl,*

my little brother, my partner, my Wolferl,
my villain, my rascal, my Wolfgang Amadè!

> *could I have done?*

The Baroness: Die Freiherrin von Berchtold zu Sonnenburg

Nannerl Mozart on Finding an Ivory
of the Wunderkinder

Found in a trunk, this old medallion—
whoever holds it in her palm

is observed by two children in miniature.
The girl rests one hand on his sweet shoulder,

the other clasps a music notebook to her
white breast. The boy offers the bit of color,

a reddish-gray jacket—the plumage
of a male against the female décolletage.

She, the older,
born on a midnight midsummer,

he, the younger,
born in the ice of new year.

Mother's *Bube* and Father's *Mädl,*
children worth keeping eternal

stare from a nest, modest as marriage,
turtle doves kept in an ivory cage

where all goes well, as it's written to be.
Eat, little ones, shit daintily,

hop and sing. Do not look at my old face
with such wide-eyed silence.

On the Prefect's Death

Of the men in my life,
the Prefect was the kindest,
never giving me reason

to hope. Now I must swallow
this prescription, take it
morning and evening followed

by the remainder of days
and repeated as
necessary to keep

moving. I tell
my hand everything
will be fine.

It mustn't demand,
mustn't act up,
mustn't be frightened.

Must be gracious when it receives
a slight card—
elegant condolences

from my sister–in–law—
mustn't betray any weakness
in sorrow or freedom.

A Promise Remembered

—N. Mozart on her daughter's death

Theater will be better than reading *Sir Grandison,*
I told her, over the half-packed trunk.
She stared at me with eyes too old for twelve;
after her father's death, hiding the glare.
You'll see, Jeanette, I said. You'll love it—
living in Salzburg, attending the Hoftheater...

in the lobby, the stench of Occupation:
horse urine, tobacco, French after-dinner farts,
uniforms stained in sweat and almond
wig powder. "Perform, perform!"
The troupe tried; the General croaked louder
and jumped the ingénue in her dressing room.

Who won when the French marched home?
Musicians and scientists fled East
to look for work. And beg in Vienna's parks.
Half Salzburg burned. In the flames
panic squawked in smoke-gagged streets,
mouthing my promise, *You'll love it.* A chasm

opened at your feet, issuing a lava
of bone, blood, ash, lice, loss. Ghosts'
laughter tumbled loose with no script
or sense of timing. This was not the theater
I meant to show you. To whatever was left,
your eyes, dear Jeanette, went blind.

Nannerl Mozart Attends the Funeral
of the Archbishop

So it was I, Wolfgang, who lived to see him dead,
the man who considered the anatomy of a woman and found it
unsuitable to sit at an organ. Did he even know our name?
Those Mosars, Mozarti, Morsach, Mooarsch, Missorts, Mozrats.
A snap of his fingers brought dozens of musicians, hungry to flock
to an audience to play for him in Salzburg. Shit birds, all of us
though he was not above reading our notes, the personal
letters he and his agents confiscated—did he recognize
the false names we used like children to outwit him?

Archbooby without a see. Gave it up before the French
marched into Salzburg. Hardly a candle lit for him in St. Peter's.
Well, we cheated him, too. Giving neither lip service nor loyalty.
Sic transit gloria mundi. After a while the taste of death fills
and one forgets, Wolfgang. Though I shall never forget his face,
a face no mother could love, a face a wife itches to slap.
A face soured on dishes of sugar, on almonds served by hands
more generous than his own. Not one shadow visited his eyes,
entering the fog like a sad man who wanted to change.

Nannerl Mozart: On Her Sister-in-Law's Garden

My dear nephew Wolfgang tells me his mother's garden is lovely.
Perhaps. What does she grow? Bantam lieutenants from Baden?
Crowing *Constanze*! in their white uniforms? I ask; he ignores my
muttering. Wolfgang's ear is more selective than his mother's.

Little gardens, I remind him, are a learned accoutrement
for someone well acquainted with alleys, a success
of the ragman who dies with a tin of coffee on his shelf.
And the room paid for. "Come," he says, "we'll go visit her."

Walk half way up the Nonnberg? Too far for me at my age.
He proposes rests along the way. I say I've never cared for views.
"But hers is most excellent," he rhapsodizes, ever the loyal son,
"one looks out over the Salzach, over its changing seasons."

Whatever does a young man know of changing seasons?
Can he imagine an old woman's?—A summer afternoon's?
Long ago Katherl and I, hot from a pilgrimage up Salzburg's
old lanes to the Church of Maria Plain. Our blood pounded.

On the bench under the chestnut tree we caught our breath,
endured the cornflowers' and wild poppies' cloysome caroling
and the ostinato drill of bees. Katherl, dear blockhead, inspired
by nature, was ready to open her legs to any lover.

— Paperlight?
Yes, Wolfgang, I am that! An object wind dismisses in a garden;
you'd have to tie me to a kite string. Better for a stay-at-home

like me to rattle among old friends—my dark Rembrandt
and Van Dyke. My della Croce. Your father's clavier

where I interpret my own seasons—
a left hand that knows the time but is weak
in following, a right hand that finds, in the silence
on the opposite side, the lost possibility of duet.

Walking to Mass

Whose eyelashes curled in from crying?
Hard for me to remember—over
which death? In the end one
gives up, blind from seeking
the cause of why, an ache
in motion, numbness when
standing still. I pause
while the world settles—
with calmer heartbeat—
into the sweet gallery
of the mass—Kyrie,
Gloria, Credo, Sanctus,
Benedictus, Agnus Dei—
oh, see, old eyes; yes, you see!

Feeling the Way

Stench of stale beer. Wooden barrel rolling thunder:
The blind woman's passing the *Stiftskeller* door.
Feels a rush of cool air from the cellar stairwell,
Down where round-faced monks work in the gloom.
She hears the voices of seven white moons
Waxing and waning—

Now she has felt her way to the park.
Smell of brew and chestnut.
Afternoon is a safe time to sit,
Before lawn bowlers begin to drink.
Under the spreading *Kastanien*—
their white blossoms in June still blooming—
The old woman's shadow slips
Into the shade of an ancient bride.

On the Staircase to #8 Hannibalplatz

A door, ajar, a glimpse
into the room on the third floor, inside,
window light and fixed positions,
where the table always stood,
where the meal always steamed,
where kreuzer racked our talk—
giving up coffee to save a florin,
making soles last with paper and wood,
darning stockings and re-darning:
a concentration on stitching
together the impossible.
No lure in this memory.
Yet the mesmerism of its being
behind a door—ajar—to a room
where the dead once spoke—
I see them so clearly!
Even the crumb on their floor is gold
and the spoon near the bowl
no one can pick up.

Sunning in the Courtyard

Neighbors passing through the courtyard
greet *la vieille*, the clavierist, the former
prodigy, Mozart's sister, a shell washed up
on the shore, no, a snail advancing under
the arch of the last century toward a bench
at the stucco wall. Her place to sit and sun.
Die Freiherrin von Berchtold zu Sonnenburg.
The blind one, the widow, the aunt, the dark
sack of silk and wool and hair, the distant
mother and teacher, the moon with wig
threadbare in May sunlight. *La Madame
de Sonnenburg.* Nannerl. In her lap
her hands can't lie still, an old habit, to
play, or pluck at a thread, to marvel
at the continual length of an unraveling—
she woke again this morning—to wind
it around her finger and wait for the brief
show of resistance when snapped off.

The Visit

—the English couple, Vincent and Mary Novello, visit
bedridden Nannerl Mozart, July 15, 1829

they will not forget
(they wrote it in their journals)
how they brought her a birthday gift
a fortnight early (flowers? wine?),
how pleased the old woman was,
the broken shape, once the little girl
in the painting above the bed

they will remember her
efforts to speak, out
of excitement to show them
the excellent instrument—
"Yes, yes, you may play it!"—
although she no longer could play, not even
a favorite, Wolfgang's "O cara armonia"

(she had wanted to practice
for *die Engländer*, for their visit;
her nephew, Wolfgang's son,
offered to carry her in his arms
to the cembalo but the voyage was
too long for her; mid-room, he'd had
to return the nightshift of bones)

back in London, the Novellos
will listen to the Requiem

in the Portuguese Embassy chapel
they will remember her
hands, how like theirs
they'd wanted to touch again
what Wolfgang had

Crossing the Border

"...before I cross the border from which no traveler returns."

—Nannerl Mozart

One hand on the clavier remembers
How it was. Her right hand. Her left is
Held down by the weighted silence
Of a useless arm. It wants to float
Over the bass, the ocean where streams
Emerge, flow north and recede
Back into fathoms, but not
One octave can she bridge.

The right hand hangs on
Like a tough old woman,
Though the fingers slip
Over shells and ocean floor,
Though the thing that leapt—part
Girl, part fish, part father—waves *Come.*

Chronology

July 30/31, 1751: Maria Anna, "Nannerl," Mozart is born at midnight in Salzburg. She is the fourth of seven children born to Leopold and Anna Maria Mozart; only she and the seventh child survive.

1762–1769: Nannerl tours with her family throughout Western Europe and England.

1769: Too old to be a Wunderkind and with family funds not large enough to promote her career and Wolfgang's, Nannerl is retired to Salzburg. Wolfgang is fourteen; she watches her brother's career continue with tours to Italy. Her work eventually consists of giving music lessons, editing, copying manuscripts for Wolfgang, housekeeping, etc.

1773: The Mozart family moves from the Getreidegasse to #8 Hannibalplatz, near the Ballhaus Theatre.

1775: Nannerl escapes the boredom of Salzburg briefly for the opening of *La Finta giardiniera* in her favorite city, Munich.

1777: Wolfgang leaves Salzburg to tour with Mamma; at their departure Nannerl "weeps bitterly"; suffers with headache and vomiting.

1781: Wolfgang writes to Nannerl from Vienna asking about her relationship to Captain Franz Armand d'Ippold, Director of the Collegium Virgilianum in Salzburg, a school for boys. D'Ippold has caught her eye; he is a frequent visitor at the Mozart house. Wolfgang encourages his sister to marry him and move to Vienna. Leopold objects, saying d'Ippold's position cannot support his daughter.

July 3, 1778: Mamma, Anna Maria Mozart, née Pertl, dies (at 58) while chaperoning Wolfgang in Paris.

August 4, 1782: Wolfgang marries Constanze Weber in Vienna. A day after the wedding two letters arrive from Leopold. One gives his consent; the other lists objections.

August 23, 1784: Nannerl marries Johann Baptist von Berchtold zu Sonnenburg, baron and prefect of St. Gilgen, the post her grandfather Pertl had held. Their marriage of convenience comes with a contract and five surviving children from Berchtold's previous two marriages.

July 25, 1785: Leopoldus Alois Pantaleon, Nannerl's first child, is born in Salzburg. He is raised by Leopold Mozart for two years.

May 28, 1787: Leopold Mozart, 68, dies on the morning of Pentecost Sunday. Captain Franz d'Ippold, Nannerl's sweetheart, writes to both Nannerl and Wolfgang of their father's death. Nannerl returns to Salzburg to take care of the estate.

March 22, 1789: Johanna Maria Anna Elisabeth, "Jeanette," Nannerl's daughter, is born in St. Gilgen.

November 27, 1790: Maria Barbara, "Babette," Nannerl's last child, is born. She dies in 1791.

February 25, 1790: Captain Franz Armand d'Ippold, the man Leopold rejected as his daughter's suitor but who visited him frequently through Leopold Mozart's old age and illnesses, dies unmarried. Born c. 1730.

December 5, 1791: Wolfgang Amadeus Mozart dies.

1792, 1797–1807: Nannerl works with Wolfgang's first biographer, Schlichtegroll, and helps Breitkopf & Härtel locate copies of almost all of her brother's piano compositions. They publish Mozart's complete works (five volumes), *Gesamtausgabe,* in 1798, Leipzig.

1800: The French take Salzburg without resistance. French officers lodge in St. Gilgen.

February 26, 1801: Berchtold dies at age 65. Eight months after her husband's death, Nannerl moves back to Salzburg with her daughter Jeanette. There she resumes giving music lessons. Her son Leopold attends school. She rents rooms from friends, the Barisanis, for 200 gulden per year. Her pension from her husband is 300 per annum.

September 1, 1805: Jeanette dies.

1825: Nannerl goes blind.

1826: Nannerl retires from teaching.

1829: Vincent and Mary Novello from England visit, recording in their journals the Baroness was "blind, weak and almost incapable of speaking."

October 29, 1829: At 12:30 p.m. the Baroness Maria Anna Walburga Ignatia von Berchtold zu Sonnenburg née Mozart dies, cause of death listed as "Entkräftung"—exhaustion. She was seventy-eight.

June 16, 1840: Nannerl's son Leopold, who has pursued a military and then bureaucratic career, dies. Both his children, Henriette and Cäsar August Ernst, die before him, ending Nannerl's line.